More Comments about The LinkedIn Personal Trainer:

"I give seminars on LinkedIn to job seekers, execs in transitions, sales reps and entrepreneurs. LinkedIn is a valuable business tool and provides very useful functionality for each of those communities. In the spirit of the 'for dummies' series, Steve takes a complex application, which itself doesn't provide more than rudimentary help files, and presents the material in bite-sized, easily digestible chunks for the novice user. I would recommend it for anyone who has decided to use LinkedIn and wants to do it right from the very beginning."

Ed Callahan, Partner and Co-Founder, Momentum Technology Partners.

"You've heard of the tremendous benefits of using LinkedIn, and decided to give it a try. After joining and creating a profile – you wait for results. OR you can benefit from having Steve Tylock at your side as your "personal trainer" to help you maximize your success by creating a compelling profile that achieves results. For a fraction of the cost of one session with a personal trainer, save yourself hours of learning spread over many months, by using this book with its tips, suggestions, and exercises as you work at the computer. This book will pay off many times your financial and time investment."

Molly Kidwell, International Solutions Manager.

The LinkedIn Personal Trainer

Using LinkedIn to find, get found, and network your way to success

Steven Tylock

Tylock and Company
Rochester, New York

Table of Contents

Foreword

LinkedIn is a powerful business networking platform used by over 10 Million members.

But the question is: are members getting enough out of LinkedIn to see just how much this powerful platform can help them, their businesses, and their social causes?

As the founder of MyLinkedInPowerForum.com and many other LinkedIn-centric discussion groups, I've had the pleasure of talking with many professionals from all around the world about why LinkedIn is such a great business tool.

Thus, I'm truly happy that Steven Tylock has patiently written a wonderful book that can help even the newest LinkedIn user get immediate benefits from the power within LinkedIn.

What I personally like about LinkedIn Personal Trainer is what is too often left out of books on professional networking: exercises.

Exercises help us get a feel for the things we learn - much as learning to ride a bicycle is accomplished by practice, not just instruction.

Readers who complete the exercises in LinkedIn Personal Trainer will be able to confidently use LinkedIn to address their business and career objectives. And what's more, LinkedIn Personal Trainer makes an excellent gift for friends, family members, and business associates who can use the power of LinkedIn to help them, too.

Vincent Wright
Founder MyLinkedInPowerForum

Acknowledgements

I'd like to thank my wife and family for letting me do my thing to create this book. John for working with me on all of my different projects, and Kathleen for suggesting I develop this material.

Introduction

LinkedIn can help you find, and get found by, more than 10 million members. Some of those members have spent considerable time building their profile and connection network – and get a great payback for those efforts.

Individuals at the other end of the spectrum accepted an initial invitation to begin using the service, created a profile with the most rudimentary of information, and are waiting to see the benefit.

The material in this book creates a "personal training" session that will help move you from an inexperienced user of LinkedIn to one who finds, gets found, and networks efficiently.

LinkedIn helps you network but does not network for you

Your use of LinkedIn will not magically bring you in contact with special people, but it will help build your network, organize your connections, and help you find (and reach) people you might never otherwise know of.

Results are proportional to effort

I have talked with light users of the system who don't see a return in value. Most often, I can turn the situation around and ask how much time and effort they have devoted. It is then easy to make the connection that they won't see much return without putting effort into the game.

If you're looking for a frog,
spend some time near a pond…

This book offers advice and training exercises

I developed this material working one on one with individual users who grew from a basic understanding of LinkedIn to become fully functional users.

Each section includes a thought provoking question, advice, and an exercise – helping you understand why you want to take specific actions. Your profile is just that – yours, and your unique situation means that there are no stock answers. By understanding the intent of each feature, you will be in the best position to use it effectively.

By completing each section's exercise, you will move yourself closer to your LinkedIn goals – finding, being found, and networking productively.

This material was originally part of a ninety-minute private training session – the student was not expected to complete his or her changes in that time, but could finish the exercises later. You may want to read through once and provide short answers to the exercises - returning later to fill in more and expand on your initial answers.

Tip – open a web browser to your account and follow along.

What effect will weak connections have on your ability to use the LinkedIn network?

Connections – strong ties between individuals

The first and most significant concept in LinkedIn is that of connections. Without connections (and everything that relates to them), the system would be just another "here I am" sort of site.

With the concept of connections, everything changes. Connections represent trusted relationships. Relationships that help build businesses:

- Current and past co-workers
- Respected clients
- Business partners
- Trusted suppliers and vendors

The distinction being that not every relationship you have ever had is worthy of being a connection. Would you refer a trusted partner to one of your former co-workers who did an unacceptable or merely adequate job? Of course not!

And so, as a network of trusted connections, your obligation is to include quality relationships. Relationships with individuals you would gladly introduce to others in your network - without hesitation.

You will find some LinkedIn users who believe that anyone met via one email is worthy of becoming a trusted connection. There are some specific advantages and disadvantages to this approach; my view is that the disadvantages outweigh the advantages. See Appendix A for more on this.

Action: Identify several individuals whom you trust:

_____

_____

_____

How often will you be found with an empty profile?

Profile – a rich description of an individual

Not just any profile – *your profile!* This is the one place where you have complete control over how you are presented to the LinkedIn public.

While not a résumé, you want to include much of what is often put into a résumé:

- Summary of your professional history
- Specialties
- Current position
- Highlights from your career
- Significant volunteer activities
- Publications
- Education
- Special activities

By including a rich description of your skills, interests, and positions - both current and past, you increase the likelihood that other will find you!

Provide information that gives someone a good reason talk to you. (And isn't it more enjoyable to talk to someone who is interesting and active?)

Action: Note interesting portions of your background. Include activities where you work with others:

_____

_____

_____

_____

What happens when you send people a note and they <u>don't</u> see your message, but you think they have?

The LinkedIn "Home"

The *Home* tab is the starting point when you log in to LinkedIn. It provides a summary of current events, activities, and connectedness.

Inbox

The inbox holds requests – Introductions, Invitations, and other items. (In general, you will want these to be sent to your regular email address, but in case your email is lost, you can find them all here) Should you attempt to invite someone and the email address is incorrect (they no longer have that address, or you mistyped it), you will find a message to that effect here.

Inside the Inbox are folders for each of the LinkedIn activities: InMail and Introductions, Invitations, Jobs, Recommendations & Network Updates.

Action: Take action on items in your Inbox. Do you need to follow up with any of those contacts to move things along?

_____

_____

_____

_____

_____

_____

_____

What kinds of people will be receptive when you reach out?

Network Updates

Who in your network are asking questions, adding connections, updating their profiles, and hiring?

Questions have their own tab (and are explained in detail later), but LinkedIn shows a couple here as a teaser - to get you interested.

It is nice to see which of your contacts are "growing" their network. The system tells you who has been adding connections recently.

When LinkedIn users update their profiles significantly, the system will "update" the people they connect with, letting them know that something has changed.

> Tip: You may not want to update *your* network when you make small changes. You can use the setting in "Account & Settings" under "Profile Updates" to have the system notify your connections only when you tell it to.

LinkedIn also presents some job openings that the system wants you to be aware of – like the answers section, it is intended to make sure that you know the feature exists, and see that there is activity (and is also explained later).

Action: Which of your current connections are actively adding connections? Could any of the people they connect to also be your connections?

How much larger is a network where everyone has 30 connections instead of 20?

(It's not 50%)

(20x20x20 = 8000)
(30x30x30 = 27000)
(That's 237% larger!)

Just Joined LinkedIn, Your Network, and Your Groups

Below the network activity area is a section devoted to helping you build your network. If you've worked at an organization, LinkedIn wants to make it easy for you to reconnect with individuals who also worked there. To help, they show you who else lists that employer – you can review the list and reconnect to the people you recognize and worked with.

After you have completed the initial effort to add these members, the system will let you know that "5 more people" from an organization have started using LinkedIn – to let you review their names as well.

Your Network is just that – a review of your network and reach. These numbers grow as you and the people in your network add connections. It can become a bit of an incentive to break into the next level (Yeah! Fifty connections!-).

Your Groups provides a quick jumping off point for you to work with group membership (more on this later).

Action: Click the "View All" button in "Your Network". Consider how far you "reach" geographically. Do any of the industries that you reach into surprise you?

_____

_____

_____

_____

What do you want to be found for?

My Profile

Your profile is your public face on LinkedIn. It presents your professional experiences, accomplishments, and interests. By professional, I mean those activities that drive your business, income, and relationships – as well as hobbies and passions that you believe will provide a connection to others. I include orienteering in my profile because it is a passion, and I am not the only local person to do so!

When viewing the top section of this tab on LinkedIn, it lists summary information from the areas below. You can use the buttons to edit directly, or can scroll down and see those areas in more detail.

Summary

This section includes *headline*, *industry*, *summary*, and *specialties*. The headline is the single thing that you want to say about yourself to everyone who finds you – think about this carefully.

The other entries describe your abilities more fully and give you a soapbox to stand on. Use them to paint a picture of yourself and what you are looking for. I saw one enterprising profile where a sales person listed his specific successes under the specialties section.

> **Tip**: When writing for LinkedIn text boxes, compose inside the word processor of your choice (in a plain font with no special formatting) and paste into the LinkedIn box – you'll be able to check spelling and sentence structure in your word processor.

Action: List the top five "key value propositions" in your current situation. Make sure they end up inside the summary section in one form or another.

Would you rather be involved with someone who has a boring history or an interesting story?

Experience

This is the place to list your experiences. I suggest you include all of the official, unofficial, and volunteer roles you have had. If the only position you list is your current one, how useful are you to other people?

By listing all of the organizations you have had a significant involvement with, you gain the ability to be "found" for all of them as well as the ability to have others recommend you for your good work together (more on that later).

You don't need your entries to look like they came from your résumé – explain in business terms what you did and what you accomplished. Give a searcher a reason to ask you about your days building the XYZ product!

> **Tip**: You don't need to mention a short term engagement that doesn't have any real significance; and if you'd rather not list dates, don't. LinkedIn displays the data it gets, and years work fine (or no date information at all works fine).

Action: Identify the significant organizations you have worked for – both in the past and currently. Update your profile to include them.

How close were the bonds you formed in school?

Are those individuals on LinkedIn?

Education

List your school(s) and degree(s). If you have extra involvement on or off campus, you can add it to one of the "notes" sections.

Perhaps you have some specialty training. This might make a great place for mentioning your "Six-Sigma" or "Project Management Professional" training.

Other training you've had may be more focused on an industry or skill. Whatever it is, you're options are open.

Action: Update your LinkedIn "Education" profile.

Of all the great things that have ever been said about you by great people, can any of your new contacts easily "see" them?

What would you think of a LinkedIn member who had hundreds of connections but no endorsements?

Recommended By

When you are looking to begin a relationship with an individual, you like seeing that someone else has endorsed the work of the person you are considering, don't you? You're happy to let others know about the good works of people you trust, correct? Others are happy to do the same for you, right?

So let's get going!

Recommendations are a great way to establish that you are trusted and trusting. It is a step forward along the path of relationship building, and LinkedIn wants to help you do it.

You want to recommend your trusted contacts, and you want to ask for their recommendations as well. While it is often true that recommendations are reciprocal, they needn't be.

> **Tip**: You have full control over recommendations. When they are initially offered, you must approve and determine whether each is visible. Should someone submit one with a typo, or say something in an awkward way, ask them to resubmit it and offer a correction.

Action: Identify three people whom you can recommend, and three whom you can ask for recommendations:

_____

_____

_____

_____

_____

_____

Do you like to work with interesting people? Do you think others like to work with interesting people?

Additional Information

Note all of the things you are involved in that fall outside the classical boundaries of employment. Subheadings include: Websites, Interests, Groups & Associations, and Honors & Awards.

This makes a good spot to include your civic, youth, artistic, volunteer, and otherwise fun endeavors. (Of course, if you spend enough time on something that it looks like a job, you might add it as a job above)

As an example – I am not the only person in the Rochester area who considers their involvement in Orienteering worth mentioning. While not a deal-maker, it may give me something else to talk about with a new contact.

Action: What additional items about yourself should you mention in your profile?

_____

_____

_____

_____

_____

_____

_____

*If someone wanted to get in touch
with you to discuss a business deal,
would you want that message delayed?*

Contact Settings

This section describes which opportunities you are interested in hearing about and how you should be contacted.

LinkedIn is interested in making the "right" connections. If you don't want to hear about job offers, you shouldn't! By the same token, you should take others' settings into consideration when you contact them.

Set these as wide as you are comfortable with, and make sure that you hear about items quickly – direct email to your regular account.

Action: Determine what contact types you are interested in, and set your profile accordingly.

_____

_____

_____

_____

_____

_____

_____

How do you rate others when you see errors in the materials they write?

Profile Completeness & View as others see it

This tab includes a button at the top that allows you to view your profile as other see it. Use this page to proof your layout.

You may also want to ask one of your close contacts to review your profile and give you feedback (truly seeing it as others see it). Be sure to ask someone that you trust to give you a critical review, a mere acquaintance or family member will likely say that it looks nice...

LinkedIn has a gauge to determine whether users have filled out their profile. This is an arbitrary meter that considers how many of the areas you have completed, and how many jobs you have entered. If it acts as an incentive to get you to keep working at building your profile, great. If it bothers you, ignore it.

Action: View your profile and note what needs to be cleaned up.

_____

_____

_____

_____

_____

_____

_____

This is another place to ask yourself:
how do I want to be found?

Public Profile (Web)

LinkedIn offers a version of your profile over the web for anyone to see. The contents of that profile are completely up to you!

The *Edit My Public Profile* tab allows you to exercise that control. It also allows you to claim a web page for your profile.

This web page makes a great addition to your signature! Would you rather be:

http://www.linkedin.com/pub/0/301/b1a

or

http://www.linkedin.com/in/stevetylock

You may review the sections of your profile that can be made available to determine what you'd like to release.

Note: the information in your public profile *will* be indexed by Google!

Tip: Edit "Your Public Profile URL" and claim a human readable page, add that URL to your email signature.

Action: What sections of your profile do you want released to the web?

_____

_____

_____

_____

_____

_____

If your LinkedIn profile is the best description of yourself, doesn't it make sense to call it to people's attention?

Email Signatures

The "Email Signatures" link (under My Profile) offers an area in which you can build a snappy signature. The tool includes areas for all the different types of information LinkedIn thinks people put in signatures, and allows you to specify one of several layouts.

I prefer a simple signature that can be expressed without formatting, but the great thing about it is that you are free to select according to your own preferences!

Action: Select the information you would like in your signature and use the LinkedIn email signature tool to create your new signature.

_____

_____

_____

_____

_____

_____

_____

Have you maximized your ability to be found based on your profile?

Findability

Profiles are parsed by LinkedIn to make it easy for members to find contacts. These searches (explained in detail later) reach into your profile for key words and names.

For example, if you want to find a consultant specializing in turning around IT infrastructures, you can type "turnaround IT consultant" into the keyword search window and get results.

How do you get found for your specialty? Mention it in your profile! You can't be found for something you don't mention!

Action: Review your profile one last time to find out whether you have everything you want in there. Search for yourself using common keywords and see if your profile comes up! List additional steps you will take over the next 30 days to increase your reach:

_____

_____

_____

_____

_____

_____

Do you have an easy way (outside of LinkedIn) to see what your network connections have been up to recently?

My Contacts

You reach into the LinkedIn world through your contacts. You "see" three levels of information: your contacts (1), their contacts (2), and the contacts of your contacts' contacts (3). In addition, LinkedIn will let you see information about a limited number of people who are not "in" your network, but will hide the names of those people.

All of your connections have profiles and connections of their own.

The *My Contacts* page lists each of your connections and includes a graphic that displays the size of their network (with a tan ring if they have recently added to it).

Connection's Profiles

I Hope your connections have taken as much time to build their profile as you have!

Their profiles will fill in information that you might not be aware of such as other positions, specialties, and interests.

Not only can you review their profiles individually, you can use the LinkedIn search tool to find individuals in your network who meet certain criteria (more on searching later).

Action: List three companies that you'd like to learn that you have a connection to:

_____

_____

_____

What's larger, connecting to 100 people who each connect to 20 more or connecting to 50 people who each connect to 50?

Connection's connections

Each of your connections has connections – their own network. By default you can see you connections' names (and they can see the names of people in your network). Your network increases when your connections add to their networks.

Help your friends grow their own networks!

> **Tip:** Should you not want to reveal the names of your connections to your network, you can do so in the Account & Settings → Connections Browse area. Be careful as this is a trust issue – telling your connections that you don't trust them to see whom you connect to is a powerful message. (I only connect to people I trust, I leave my connection list open.)

Action: Look over some of your direct connections. List some of their contacts that could become your contacts (because you already know them):

_____

_____

_____

_____

_____

_____

Can you think of a situation in your environment that would lead you to want to cut off an association?

Removing connections

Sometimes you wind up with a connection that you added without realizing that you didn't know the person well, or perhaps the relationship has changed and you no longer want to list them. LinkedIn provides a mechanism to remove connections, and that silently severs the relationship.

Action: Find the "Remove Connections" dialogue on the "My Contacts" screen – click on it to see the screen that is used to remove connections.

_____

_____

_____

_____

_____

_____

_____

Was there any aspect of LinkedIn that you wondered about before you understood it better? Can you describe LinkedIn better so that your invitations don't get held up while the recipient checks it out?

Invitations

LinkedIn is all about inviting contact. You invite others already on the system to join your network. You also invite people who are not yet part of LinkedIn to join. Others will find you and invite you to join their network.

Once established, your network becomes a means to invite others into appropriate business discussions.

You'll find dialogue boxes to use to invite people on many of the screens. (Descriptions for the additional options *Other Contacts* and *Colleagues & Classmates* follow this page). At the basic level, you invite with an email address, a first name, and a last name. You add a personalized message about using LinkedIn and send it off.

> **Tip**: LinkedIn will supply a sample message for your invitation. Please personalize it. (It's your personal invitation, not spam. The canned message is not very personal)

> **Tip**: LinkedIn allows you to "mass mail" a large group of people at one time. Unless you can craft a message to the group along the lines of "I'm looking to get in touch with everyone from the Acme Development Team", you're better off sending individual invitations with a personal message.

You want to invite people to both join your network as well as join LinkedIn. The former is a bit easier. You know they use the tool and, if they remember you, the connection should follow. If they do not use LinkedIn, you need to explain the benefits: find and get found, no cost, and safety. For your network to grow, you've got to encourage people to join your network in both ways.

Action: List groups of people you'd like to invite:

_____

_____

_____

Should you invite people to connect just because you have their email addresses?

Other Contacts

LinkedIn wants you to be successful – expanding your list of connections will help make you successful.

LinkedIn can take the email addresses that you have in your email program and compare that list against the email-address-based user accounts it keeps.

Because of the prevalence of webmail (Yahoo, gmail, AOL, Hotmail) and Microsoft Outlook, LinkedIn has developed programs that work specifically with those. (If you use another mail reader you can export your contact list and import it via another mechanism.) You can find out who is already using LinkedIn!

Download the "Outlook Toolbar" under the "Tools" heading of the bottom menu.

For webmail and importing contact files, select "Sitemap" from the bottom menu and then "Find Contacts Wizard" under the "Tools" heading.

The tools are great to use, but makes it too easy to send a mass invitation to everyone who has ever sent you an email. Remember the rule about only inviting your trusted contacts? Just send out individual connection requests to the specific people you identify. It will take longer, but you will have a better network because of it.

Action: Use LinkedIn's tool to pull in your main email program's contact list – invite your close contacts who are already members of LinkedIn, and then write invitations for those who are not yet part of LinkedIn.

Is it easier to establish a connection while you work with someone, or after you have left an organization?

Colleagues & Classmates

The Colleagues & Classmates sections help you re-connect with associates from former jobs and schools.

It does this by searching for members who share the company or college that you list. You will have an opportunity to re-connect to people you know.

If you list the years you were at the company or college, LinkedIn will look for others with overlapping time periods.

> **Tip**: some people will attempt to connect to "everyone" who was at the same large company – even if they didn't know the individuals. You don't want to do that.

Action: Which former colleagues would you like to re-connect with?

_____

_____

_____

_____

_____

_____

_____

Doesn't it feel great to be invited into someone else's network?

Receiving Invitations

In the same way that you are reaching out to find your former co-workers, classmates, colleagues, and friends, others are doing the same – and they may find you before you find them!

When you receive an invitation from someone you trust, by all means accept it. (There is one caution about having multiple email addresses and potentially creating multiple LinkedIn accounts – please make sure you read the advice on multiple email addresses found on page 67.)

> **Tip**: If you don't remember someone, reply and ask the person to remind you how you knew each other.

You will also receive invitations from people you don't know. In the same way that you should not invite anyone to join your network unless you know and trust them, you should not accept invitations from anyone you don't know and trust. (Mega-Connectors are discussed more in Appendix A.)

Action: Review any open invitations in your Inbox.

_____

_____

_____

_____

If you worked at a larger organization, you might not be willing to connect to every person there, but would you feel an affinity for other ex-employees?

Groups

LinkedIn allows "group" membership. Others in the same group can see each other's profiles and get in touch – through LinkedIn.

You are not provided contact information for group members, and there are no mass-group contact methods, but it still provides a great way to reach others that share membership in the group.

Groups are strictly opt-in, and you should check to see if any alumni, ex-employee, or other networking organizations that you belong to have established a group.

If the group you want to join does not already exist you can create a new group!

Action: Note some groups that you belong to and check to see if LinkedIn has established a group for them:

_____

_____

_____

_____

_____

_____

_____

Suppose there is a company that you are looking to partner with. What resources do you have to find out about the company and the people who work there?

Now you have one more.

Search (People)

The LinkedIn search menu is the mechanism to turn your effort in building a network and creating a profile into results.

The "Search" and "Advanced Search" buttons are displayed prominently in most screens. (They duplicate the "People" tab) Learn to use them.

Keywords, Name, Title, Company: Search your network for instances of words in these specific locations of a profile.

Location, Industry, Interested In, Joined Network: Limit the search according to any of these factors.

> **Tip**: Select a country (US), a blank ZIP Code, and the "located in or near" item to restrict the search to anywhere in the US.

Sort: Present the results according to a variety of factors.

Search results present on two tabs: those within your network (up to 500) on a primary tab and those outside of your network (up to 20) on a second. If there are no results in your network, but results outside of your network exist, you will view the outside results.

Should the results include too many members, you can "Refine Search" to easily add another condition or otherwise restrict results.

When you select a profile from a search, you see that profile. Review and contact, if you wish! (see "Introductions" on page 61)

Action: Using the companies you wanted to find information about (from the "Connection's Profiles" Action), conduct searches to see what is available.

_____

_____

_____

_____

As a job searcher, how helpful is it to check into the job and poster?

As a job poster, can you see a benefit in reviewing the applicant's profile with recommendations?

Jobs & Hiring

LinkedIn provides tools to search through job postings as well as a way to post openings (for a fee).

For those looking for a position, in addition to jobs posted in LinkedIn, the site partners with Simply Hired to list positions discovered over the web.

When you find a position posted on LinkedIn, not only will you find a person posting the position, you have a built-in path of trusted network connections to reach that person! It is possible for a position to be posted without contact information – in that case, use the search tool to find who in your network works at the target company. Ask your trusted connection for a referral for the opening! Ask about the company and the people there!

For those with job openings to fill, you can check out your candidates! This is better than looking up information on applicants that come with a résumé and cover letter. In addition to the online profile and recommendations, you can find other LinkedIn members who have worked with the companies noted. ("Reference Search" under the *People* tab is a simplified, fee based tool to help you do this. Without paying, you can still search for contacts that list the same employers as your applicant has listed.)

Action: Look up several jobs that you might be interested in looking at or would be similar to positions you need to fill.

_____

_____

_____

_____

_____

Would you like to be listed when people on the network search for resources in your service sector?

Services (recommended service providers)

The *Services* tab allows members to find service providers that have been recommended by others in the network. The results can be limited to specific service groups, 1st level connections, 1st and 2nd level connections, or all LinkedIn users.

As someone who is looking for services, you can use this tab to find people who are specifically recommended.

As someone who wants to be found, you want to be recommended by your clients and customers – so that you show up in this area when others search!

Action: Plan how you will get recommendations so that you will be listed here.

_____

_____

_____

_____

_____

_____

_____

Would you like to ask something of your network?

Would you like to answer a question from someone in your network?

Answers

LinkedIn added the "Answers" section to allow members to ask and answer business related questions. It is the only method available to "reach" your entire network and, as such, it is prone to abuse (as users learn how to get value from it).

Your question or answer is widely seen; so take care to make sure it reflects well on you.

Please don't use the section to "troll" for contact.

It is ok to recruit, advertise, or announce you are looking for a job - but please follow the guidelines.

This area is ignored by some users, and loved by others. Your participation is up to you and your comfort level.

Action: Click into the Answers section and see if there are any questions posed that you'd like to answer (and do so).

Would you look to see what changed if one of your network connections added a job?

Announcements

Two events allow you to send out an announcement – updating your profile and letting people know about a job.

The default setting for LinkedIn has a message automatically sent to your direct contacts when you do something major to your profile like add a new job. I prefer more control over that, and have altered the settings in Account & Settings → Profile Updates to manually send those notices out.

To send out a specific announcement, I use the "Forward" button on the top of "My Profile" to send an announcement.

When I am asking my contacts for simple job referrals, I can go to the "InBox" and "Send a message" about a "job notification". That brings me to a screen where I can type in a short message as well as an overview of the job opening.

Either of these items can be prone to abuse or overuse – moderation is a good thing!

In the same way that you may want to contact others about changes in your life, they will be sending you notices of their own.

Action: Plan updates so that your network will see what is happening in your career and business.

Would you agree to contact if one of your trusted friends recommended the other party to you?

Connecting through Introductions!

Outside of searching, the other significant benefit from your network is the ability to contact other LinkedIn members. You may want to discuss a new business opportunity, a partnership, a job, a reference, or a sale – the potential is limitless and entirely up to you!

The special aspect of this contact is that it is via a chain of mutual trusted connections.

Let's say that you connect to Mary, and Mary connects to John. You'd like to contact John in order to discuss a business opportunity. While you can use LinkedIn to find out about Mary's connection to John and can always pick up the phone to talk to Mary directly, LinkedIn includes a way for you to send a message to John and route it through Mary. You might type:

> "John, I'd like to get together with you to discuss a sales opportunity with the XYZ Corporation…"

And you would also include a message to Mary:

> "Mary, I'm hoping you can connect me with John – I think we have a great business opportunity together."

Your "Get Introduced" message goes first to Mary – she sees both your message to John and to her and has the chance to approve or deny the message. Because members generally trust each other, the inclination is to make worthwhile requests and to approve them. But, if Mary does not approve the message, John never sees it.

If she approves the message, she forwards the original along with her own addition:

> "John, I've worked with Steve for several years - you'll want to make the time to talk with him."

John then sees Mary's recommendation and the original message (but not the message to Mary).

Do you have better success when you are introduced to your new clients by your existing clients?

It is possible to send a message to a third degree connection as well. Each person in the chain must approve and forward the request.

By building the communication stream through trusted connections, weak requests will not get through. (Should one of my friends get involved with a multi-level marketing system, I'm not likely to pass those requests through to my other close connections.)

When multiple connection paths reach your target, you decide which of your contacts it should start through. Send your message over a route that is 2 levels deep in preference to 3 levels, and otherwise choose your contact with the best relationship.

You can follow the approval path of your request. In the Inbox area, select "Sent" InMail & Introductions, and click on the specific introduction you'd like to review.

Action: Plan a connection attempt with a contact you want to get to know better.

_____

_____

_____

_____

_____

_____

Compare the level of trust you would assess for messages that come from
 a) a trusted contact,
 b) an InMail, or
 c) an unsolicited email
Does InMail provide a leg up versus an unsolicited email?

Upgrading your account and InMail

LinkedIn understands that connection attempts three levels deep may be less likely to work out – and that they will take extra time to reach the final connection.

To help provide quick connections, they developed InMail. InMail has a feature that lets one member contact another member directly, without the use of the introduction network. This feature can also be used to contact others who are outside of their network.

For example, if you're a recruiter, this is very helpful if you're searching for people based on their profiles.

The use of InMail requires an upgraded account or purchase of one or more units of InMail. The account levels offer different monthly quantities of InMail messages, and InMails may be purchased on the Accounts & Settings page.

If you don't need to contact people like this, the standard (free) account works quite well.

Configuring your account to receive InMail is accomplished on the Account & Settings → Contact Settings tab. You can decline all InMail if you prefer, and so can other members.

Action: Jot down some situations where you might like to get in touch with someone through LinkedIn with an InMail:

_____

_____

_____

_____

_____

_____

Do you use more than one
email address?

Multiple Email Addresses

The most common problem individuals have asked me to help fix is that of having multiple LinkedIn accounts.

An individual generally does not understand how it happens, but the following story illustrates it – if you remember that your email address defines your account name.

> John Smith (jsmith@somecompany.com) starts using LinkedIn, creates an initial profile with basic information, and invites a half dozen trusted contacts. Things are working well.
>
> Later that week John's good friend Sally notices that John is using LinkedIn and says "Hey, John's in now. I better invite him!"
>
> Sally thinks John has a personal email at jsmith@someISP.com and uses that when LinkedIn asks for an email address.
>
> LinkedIn knows that those two "accounts" are different and sends off a new invitation to the new John Smith.
>
> John reads the email at home and thinks "This is great! I'm expanding my network already!"
>
> He doesn't realize that he is creating a new account for this new email address when he clicks on the link.
>
> Six months later someone points out that there are two John Smiths in the system and they both look like alike!

Protect yourself from having this happen – under Account & Settings → Email Addresses, register all of the email addresses that you use (work and home).

If you already have multiple accounts, pick one as "the best" and consolidate into it. Re-invite anyone not connected to it and copy and paste any text you have typed into the odd account(s). After doing this, send an email to LinkedIn support asking them to remove the odd account(s). (and register all of your email addresses as above)

Action: Search for yourself on LinkedIn – take action if you have multiple accounts. Register all of your valid email addresses.

Do you see now how you can find, get found, and network your way to success with LinkedIn?

Wrapping Things Up

All training sessions start with a motivated student who has a goal: getting better at this task. The LinkedIn Personal Trainer creates a training environment for you every time you pick it up – you're the student, and the goal is to get more out of LinkedIn.

Find

Find based on what you're looking for, what's in other people's profiles, and who you connect to. The more precise your search, the more information others have in their profiles, and the larger your network - the better results you'll find.

Get Found

You get found based on what's in your profile and whom you connect to. The more information you have, and the larger network you are a part of - the more you'll get found.

and Network

Keep in touch and take small actions to stay connected to people you enjoyed being with. Build and maintain connections that will serve you for a lifetime. It's not what or who you know, or even who knows you, it's how well your network runs.

Your Way

By now you realize that there is no formula for success. Your life: your contacts, your activities, your skills and strengths – everything that makes you "you" – is unique. By understanding how LinkedIn works, you will be set to work with it in your own way.

To Success

It is out there, and my hope is that this guide puts you one step closer to reaching your goals in life. LinkedIn is one tool that can help you along your way.

Have you checked out
www.linkedinpersonaltrainer.com?

Action:
Go and use LinkedIn!

If part of your success hinges on reaching as many people as possible, can you see why a large network full of weak connections might work for you?

Appendix A: Mega-Connectors

A product is successful when it is being used in ways that the original creators never intended. That happens with LinkedIn.

Throughout this guide, I have referred to *trusted contacts*, emphasizing that you will connect to, recommend, refer, match and otherwise work with your *trusted* contacts.

That model works very well, but is not the only model.

Some individuals believe that the best network is the largest network. They don't care about knowing the people they are connected to, just that they are connected.

This gives them a network that has an extensive reach – thousands of first level connections, millions of third level.

With this network, they are able to search extensively.

It comes with a downside though. When faced with a request to introduce people, recommend, or otherwise interact, they may not know either party. A forward reference through them is half-hearted or well-meaning at best, and does not assure either party that the other can be trusted. And given the extensive network that they have, they may well be inundated with requests – and unable to keep up.

It reminds me of the restrictions on the Genie in Disney's *Aladdin* – Phenomenal cosmic powers! Itty-bitty living space…

Index

About the Author

Steve Tylock is an Information Technology Executive, Strategist, Creative Thinker, Author, Speaker, Husband, Father, and Child of God. He says so right on his LinkedIn profile:

http://www.linkedin.com/in/stevetylock

His professional experience includes supporting IT infrastructure from early system administration roles through team leadership, management, and overall technology direction. He has consulted in education, product development, manufacturing, government, small and large business environments.

His love of singing and community theater has put him on and off stage for a number of years; he is currently performing with the Traveling Cabaret. He has fun orienteering (running with a purpose) in the parks of Western New York, and has equal enjoyment skiing when snow is on the ground. Other interests include scouting, boating, hiking, fishing, golfing, and most any manner of game playing.

The youngest of six himself, Steve and his wife raise their four children in a suburban home that also includes various family pets and temporary guests of all sizes.

Printed in the United States
213464BV00003B/124/A